PORTSMOUTH
THEN AND NOW

Compiled and photographed
by
ANTHONY TRIGGS

MILESTONE PUBLICATIONS

Published by Milestone Publications,
62 Murray Road, Horndean, Hampshire PO8 9JL

British Library Cataloguing in Publication Data

Triggs, Anthony
Portsmouth then and now.
1. Portsmouth (Hampshire) History
Pictorial works 2. Portsmouth (Hampshire)
Description Views
I. Title
942.2′79208′0222 DA690.P8

ISBN 0-903852-66-7

Design Brian Iles

Phototypeset by Monitor Publications Ltd, Hayling Island

Printed and bound in Great Britain by
R.J. Acford, Chichester

Jacket front: Guildhall Square, 1986.
Jacket rear: Handley's Corner, Southsea, 1932.

ACKNOWLEDGMENTS

I would like to thank Miss Alison Marshall, Mr. Ron Brown, Mr. E. Pettet, Mr. Roger Reynolds, and the B.B.C. Hulton Picture Library for their help in supplying photographs from their collections.

Thanks must also go to Mr. Russell Fox of the Portsmouth City Museum, and to Miss Sarah Brown of the library of the Royal Commission on the Historical Monuments of England.

My colleague, Maurice Hulbert, librarian at The News, and his staff also deserve my thanks, as does Mr. Steve Whale. Finally, I once more give thanks to my wife, Sue, for her continuing encouragement and help.

INTRODUCTION

A little over a year ago I compiled *Portsmouth Past and Present,* my first collection of "before and after" views of the great city of Portsmouth.

And judging from the response of the book-buyers of Portsmouth – for the first printing sold out within three weeks – it was well received.

It is very easy to look at an old photograph showing a particular part of the city, but it is a different matter to place that view into its present-day perspective. The fact that each old picture in *Portsmouth Past and Present* was matched with a modern one taken from the same viewpoint, gave readers the opportunity to compare changes at a glance.

I have now collected a further 45 old pictures, and have given them a similar treatment, for as before, each one is faced by its modern counterpart. This collection I have called *Portsmouth Then and Now.*

Nowadays there is a camera in nearly every household. Equipment can range from the most expensive state-of-the-art electronic marvel, to the simplest of pocket cameras.

But up to the turn of the century the situation was entirely different. Although a form of photography was in use by 1840, for the following 80 years or so it was still considered to be a new art, and the uses for it were being worked out while the process evolved.

So the majority of pictures, especially street scenes, were taken by the professional photographers, who usually had the intention of selling them as postcards.

The Frenchman Louis Daguerre made the first significant breakthrough into photography back in 1835, but his process – the Daguerrotype – was clumsy, and pictures needed an exposure of between 15 and 30 minutes. Pictures could not be reprinted as there was no negative.

In 1840 the English scientist and M.P., William Henry Fox Talbot, who lived at Lacock Abbey in Wiltshire, created the first practical process, producing any number of prints from an original negative.

By 1851 the wet-plate process was perfected. This system required the glass plate to be coated, sensitised, and exposed while still wet, and was a cumbersome process. The photographer had either to remain near his darkroom, or take a portable one with him.

However the wet-plate era brought a great expansion of the photographic profession. Quality was improved, and the ability to produce high-grade prints quickly and efficiently led to pictures being sold country-wide.

The invention of gelatin soon allowed the dry plate to dominate photography, and by 1888 the American George Eastman had introduced a roll-film camera, which took 100 round pictures on a single film.

Eastman was a New York bank clerk who was interested in photography, but soon grew dissatisfied with the messy, expensive, laborious process. "It seemed that one ought to be able to carry less than a pack-horse load," he was reported as saying.

His revolutionary system provided the user with a complete service. The whole camera was returned to the factory, and it came back reloaded, with 100 card-mounted prints. Eastman's slogan: "You press the button, we do the rest," captured the world, even though his service was relatively expensive.

However the art was still largely used by professionals. Eastman changed that in 1900 when his five-shilling (25p) Brownie box camera brought picture-taking to the general public, and paved the way for the modern equipment with which we are all familiar.

The contemporary photographer Alvin Langdon Coburn observed ruefully: "Now every nipper has a Brownie, and a photograph is as common as a box of matches."

In passing, I feel it is fitting to recall two photographers of the period who are mentioned by name, both in this volume and the previous one.

The first is the well-known Waterlooville photographer, Charles Herbert Taylor Marshall, who travelled the area with his bulky plate camera, recording the events of the time, especially the building of the Horndean Light Railway.

He rarely visited Portsmouth, but did photograph Cosham, which at that time was not within the town boundary. Many of his glass negatives had been saved by his daughter Alison, who very kindly allowed me to use some of them.

Another brilliant cameraman, although not local, was Francis J. Mortimer. Like Marshall, he was an innovative craftsman, specialising mainly in seascapes, and his invention of a waterproof box to protect his camera enabled him to capture some dramatic shots of the ocean.

He was editor of Amateur Photographer from 1908-1918, and again from 1925-1944. The Mortimer collection is now part of the B.B.C. Hulton Picture Library.

Finally, I would like to dedicate this book to my grandfather's brother, Frederick Thomas Triggs, who was better known to followers of local history as Richard Esmond. He wrote many articles for the then Evening News, and also published two books on the history of the city he loved. He was no mean artist, and his pen-drawn illustrations were an excellent companion to his writing.

The final sentence in his book *Portsmouth Not So Old* sums up his feelings about the city:

"With all its faults, and its failures in comparison with the wonder places of the Earth, it has a remarkable way of being first in the hearts of its natives – it is home."

Anthony Triggs
Portchester, 1986

CONTENTS

SOUTH PARADE 1877 Beach Mansions, an hotel opened in 1866, stands proudly on the waterfront at Southsea, at a time just before the building of South Parade Pier, when the area consisted mainly of Naval officers' dwellings.

(Royal Commission on the Historical Monuments of England)

SOUTH PARADE 1986 The mansions still stand, although in another guise, but the seaside resort's glitter has destroyed the tranquillity of the previous picture. The present pier was built in 1908, after a fire destroyed the original one.

LUMPS FORT 1937 Lumps Fort was built in 1539, and was sold for £47,000 to the city of Portsmouth in 1931, together with 13 acres of land, which once boasted a large farm and a windmill.

LUMPS FORT 1986 Although a bid was put in to build a fun-fair, the eventual redevelopment turned the fort area into walkways, a rose garden, and a model village, and became a popular area for holidaymakers.

CANOE LAKE 1905 This commercial postcard view shows the lake with Edwardians enjoying the sun and the water. The peaceful pleasures of the turn of the century are well illustrated in this picture. At one time the lake boasted a swannery.

CANOE LAKE 1986 The lake is still a popular venue for holidaymakers and residents alike, where youngsters can sail their boats, or feed the swans. Now high-rise flats form a modern backdrop to the view.

SOUTHSEA CASTLE 1900 This picture shows Victorians out for a stroll along the Southsea Castle foreshore. The castle was built on the orders of Henry VIII as part of his defence of the realm policy, and from it he watched the tragic sinking of the Mary Rose.

(Mr. E. Pettet)

SOUTHSEA CASTLE 1986 The castle, and its next-door neighbour the D-Day Museum, is a popular place for visitors and residents alike. The lighthouse, built in 1823 and standing 51 feet above sea level, dominates the castle, which is now a showpiece and a museum in its own right.

PALMERSTON ROAD 1936 Palmerston Road, with Handleys on the left, was a popular shopping area, and became a social mecca for the young, which led to the oft-heard cry upon parting: "See you in Palmy."

(The News)

PALMERSTON ROAD 1986 Like so many large shopping areas, Palmerston Road is now a pedestrian precinct. Its wide spaces contrast so vividly with the road shown in the opposite picture.

OSBORNE ROAD 1921 A tram, bound for the Dockyard makes its way along Osborne Road, past the Queen's Hotel. The first hotel of that name was destroyed in 1901, with the death of two chambermaids.

OSBORNE ROAD 1986 The Queen's Hotel still stands, and the buildings opposite are structurally the same. The tram poles, of course, have now disappeared.

CLARENCE BEACH 1935 The beach was a popular place in those palmy pre-war days. In the background is the outstanding Clarence Pier, which was virtually destroyed during the war.

CLARENCE BEACH 1986 The sun-worshippers are still there, and the rebuilt pier, which was opened in 1961, stands in the background. Beachwear, however, has become a lot smaller in the ensuing years.

WESTERN PARADE 1900 The extension of upper-middle class Southsea took place between 1860 and 1885. The Grosvenor Hotel was opened in the early 1880s on the site of the old Cricketers' Tavern, which stood upon Froddington Heath, now Southsea Common.

(Mr. E. Pettet)

WESTERN PARADE 1986 The ornate buildings still face out towards Clarence Esplanade. The Common, eastwards from a line drawn from Southsea Castle to the Grosvenor Hotel, was purchased by the Corporation from the War Office for £45,000.

ELM GROVE 1937 The church marked the junction of Elm Grove and King's Road, itself a busy shopping centre in the pre-war days. Just beyond the church was the Bush Hotel, where Sherlock Holmes was 'born', attended by Dr. Conan Doyle.

ELM GROVE 1986 King's Road was completely destroyed in the war, and the shape of Elm Grove was changed. The trees have gone – the one in the picture could well have been the last!

ALBERT ROAD 1900 This commercial view shows Albert Road before the building of the Kings Theatre. It is also interesting to note the original police station on the right of the picture.

(Mr. R. Reynolds)

ALBERT ROAD 1986 The Kings now dominates the centre of the view. The theatre, designed by Frank Matcham, was opened in 1907 by H.B. Irving, son of the famous Henry Irving.

COTTAGE GROVE 1930 Cottage Grove then was a thriving shopping area. The awnings denote a large number of small side-street businesses.

(The News)

COTTAGE GROVE 1986 Much of the surrounding area has been redeveloped, as Somers Town made its spread across the city. Apart from the shops on the right of the picture, Cottage Grove has completely changed.

FRATTON BRIDGE 1905 The narrowness of Fratton road is clearly shown by the interlacing tram lines. The building on the left is the Fratton Hotel, later to become a bank, which was destroyed during the Second World War.

(Mr. Ron Brown)

FRATTON BRIDGE 1986 Fratton Road was widened in 1929 at a cost of £89,000, when all the houses on the east side were set back, and the tram lines were laid as full double width.

FRATTON STATION 1925 A taxi and cabs await their fares outside the railway station at Fratton. The short-lived East Southsea Railway link ran from this station.

(The News)

FRATTON STATION 1986 This modern view shows that time has done little to alter the line of the houses in the background, although technical achievement has certainly altered the modes of transport.

VICTORIA PIER 1930 This was the first public pier to be built in Portsmouth. It was originally to be called the King William Pier, but the king's death overtook the construction, and it was renamed in 1837.

(The News)

VICTORIA PIER 1986 Clarence Pier and South Parade Pier caused the decline of the Victoria Pier, and in 1925 much of the original structure was destroyed. It is now used mainly by anglers and swimmers.

PEMBROKE ROAD 1920 This picture shows Pembroke Road between the wars, with the premises of the well-known publishing firm of Charpentier on the right. The company was founded in the mid 1800s by W.H. Charpentier, who specialised in maps and local histories.

(B.B.C. Hulton Picture Library)

PEMBROKE ROAD 1986 Charpentier's premises were destroyed by enemy action in 1941, taking with them an irreplaceable collection of illustrations of old Portsmouth. Some of the properties on the left of the previous picture have now been replaced by modern flats.

THE SQUARE TOWER 1900 This commercial view shows the Square Tower and that part of the Old Portsmouth fortifications known as the Saluting Platform. Early in the last century a semaphore, to signal ships at Spithead, was built on top of the tower.

(Mr. E. Pettet)

THE SQUARE TOWER 1986 Many of the fortifications have been preserved, and make a popular and historically-informative walk. The semaphore was superseded by a new one in the Dockyard, and by 1847 had been demolished.

BROAD STREET 1945 This view, looking across the harbour towards Gosport, shows The Union Tavern and The Coal Exchange. The area was soon to change dramatically when the Camber dock area was developed.

(Royal Commission on the Historical Monuments of England)

BROAD STREET 1986 The Union Tavern changed its name in the sixties to The Lone Yachtsman, in honour of Portsmouth's Sir Alec Rose and his epic single-handed round-the-world journey.

KING JAMES'S GATE 1850 King James's Gate was the earliest and most elaborate of the gates of Old Porsmouth. It was built in 1687, and was part of the last phase of the extension work done under the direction of Bernard De Gomme.

SITE OF KING JAMES'S GATE 1986 The gate was demolished in 1860, and the facade was re-erected in St. Michael's Road, and later in Burnaby Road, as an entrance to the Services' sports ground.

WHITE HART ROW 1950 Many of the narrow roads around this part of Old Portsmouth were demolished and rebuilt after the war. This view of White Hart Row gives an idea of the general appearance after the ravages of the blitz.

WHITE HART ROW 1986 Modern factories and maisonettes have replaced the tired old buildings, and much of Old Portsmouth has become an expensive residential area, boasting many 'character' properties.

QUAY GATE 1860 The gate was built in 1734, and gave access from the town quay at the Camber into Crown Street and King Charles Street.

SITE OF QUAY GATE 1986 The gate was demolished in 1871, and the quay now opens directly on to King Charles Street. The offices of the Department of Health and Social Security replace the old guardhouse.

HIGH STREET 1932 This picture shows one of the most famous buildings in High Street, the George Hotel, where Nelson spent his last night on British soil, before leaving for Trafalgar.

HIGH STREET 1986 The George Hotel was destroyed during the war, and a modern block of flats, called George Court in memory of the hotel, now occupies the site.

THE GUNWHARF GATE 1902 The picture shows the Gunwharf Gate dressed overall for the coronation of Edward VII. The gunwharf was commenced in 1662, and the area was enlarged and the gate rebuilt in 1807.

THE GUNWHARF GATE 1986 The gate now is more familiar as the former main entrance to H.M.S. Vernon, the Royal Navy shore establishment, which took over the area in 1923. The then Torpedo School had been housed in a number of old hulks moored in the harbour.

THE HARD 1900 H.M.S. Powerful was due in from the Boer War, and Portsmouth was celebrating. This picture, by F.J. Mortimer, shows the shops at the Hard, decorated for the occasion.

(B.B.C. Hulton Picture Library)

THE HARD 1986 The line of the buildings has remained the same, although new pieces have been added to form a successful mixture of both old and new, in this busy part of the city.

DOCKYARD GATES 1905 This commercial postcard view shows the trams and traders outside the gates of the Dockyard, awaiting members of the French Fleet.

DOCKYARD GATES 1986 The gates themselves have changed very little, but the area outside is soon to be altered with the construction of the dock to house H.M.S. Warrior.

QUEEN STREET 1942 Only one car can be seen in Queen Street on an obviously dismal day, but the old cannons buried in the road on the corners give a nautical look to what was the main road from the Dockyard to the town.

QUEEN STREET 1986 The narrow confines of Queen Street disappeared when a new road-widening programme was carried out. The area now would be totally unrecognizable to a war-time sailor returning for the first time.

UNICORN GATE 1900 The Unicorn Gate, mate of the Lion Gate, was originally one of the gates of the old town. It was built in 1778, and stood at the end of North Street, Portsea, but was removed in 1873 to become one of the gates of the Dockyard.

(Mr. E. Pettet)

UNICORN GATE 1986 The gate still stands, but is no longer a true gateway into the 'Yard. The cuts of recent years have ensured that the 'out-musters', where hundreds of workers on their way home would jam the area, will never be seen as they were in the period following the war.

BONFIRE CORNER 1936 There are many theories about the naming of Bonfire Corner. The most popular is that years ago the Dockyard workers were allowed to burn their waste materials on this piece of land outside the Dockyard walls.

(The News)

BONFIRE CORNER 1986 After the destruction of the second world war, council flats and houses were built on the site. However, a visitor to the area can still see the Bonfire Corner road sign high on the Naval Base wall.

LION GATE 1850 The overspill from Old Portsmouth developed on Portsea Common in the 18th Century, and two gates were built in the enclosing wall – The Lion Gate and The Unicorn Gate.

SITE OF LION GATE 1986 Lion Gate was demolished in 1871, and was rebuilt into the Semaphore Tower in the Dockyard. Lion Terrace still remains as a reminder of the past.

VICTORIA PARK 1900 The band plays on the bandstand, and this picture by F.J. Mortimer depicts exactly how the young people of the turn of the century took their leisure on what is obviously a sunny day.

(B.B.C. Hulton Picture Library)

VICTORIA PARK 1986 The park is still a haven from the bustle of the busy city streets. The bandstand, sadly, has 'isappeared, and has been replaced by a memorial. It is interesting to note the changed profile of the Guildhall.

GUILDHALL SQUARE 1939 This view shows the wide-open space of the Guildhall Square as it was. The famous Sussex Hotel stands to the left, on the corner of Greetham Street. In the centre of the picture is the tram shelter.

GUILDHALL SQUARE 1986 The Guildhall Square redevelopment makes it almost impossible to duplicate the previous viewpoint. The glass and steel of the Civic Offices and the new library building enclose the smaller present-day area.

THE GUILDHALL 1900 This view of the Guildhall, opened in 1890, was taken from Park Road, which in those days led from the square to the old Gunwharf Gate, now H.M.S. Vernon.

THE GUILDHALL 1986 The college building on the left was built in 1908, and the road has now been renamed King Henry 1 Street. Park Road now stops at Anglesea Road.

COMMERCIAL ROAD 1934 At the right of the picture, standing on the corner of a narrow Arundel Street, are the premises of the Landport Drapery Bazaar. A tram is making its way along the road, although by this time they were being phased out.

COMMERCIAL ROAD 1986 Commercial Road is now a pedestrian precinct. The L. D. B. store was destroyed during the war, and the new premises were opened in 1955. The store is now part of a national chain.

HAMPSHIRE TERRACE 1933 The tram lines and trolley cables stretch away down the terrace towards the Victoria Hall, which was the first cinema in Portsmouth.

HAMPSHIRE TERRACE 1986 The terrace frontages seem little changed, although the hall has disappeared and the high-rise Polytechnic building now dominates the skyline.

COMMERCIAL ROAD 1955 This, the youngest of the 'before' pictures in the series shows the Emperor of India public house, which stood in Commercial Road, on the corner of Paradise Street. The policeman on point duty now belongs to a bygone age.

(Portsmouth City Museum)

COMMERCIAL ROAD 1986 Much of Commercial Road is now a precinct, and shops have replaced the old pub. Paradise Street, however, still runs behind the shops, although it is now no longer residential.

MILE END CEMETERY 1954 The imposing pillars of the Mile End cemetery entrance dominate the scene. Later the cemetery was levelled, and the area made into a public park.

SITE OF MILE END CEMETERY 1986 Any trace of the cemetery and park is now lost beneath the access roads of the Portsmouth Ferry Terminal, which has changed the face of that part of the city.

LONDON ROAD 1950 This picture shows St. Mark's church, which was consecrated in 1874, and was demolished in 1970. A new St. Mark's was built just around the corner in Derby Road.

LONDON ROAD 1986 The site of the church is now covered by a modern commercial development, which has brought new life into the once-ailing shopping centre.

NORTH END 1929 By this time the bus office had replaced 'The Poplars', the house which once stood on the site. The Brunswick Dye Works opposite were soon to be demolished.

NORTH END 1986 The west side of London Road looks remarkably unchanged from the previous picture, although the buildings on the east side have disappeared, along with the trolley cables.

COPNOR CROSSING 1900 During the 1880s there was considerable pressure for a station at this point. A Station Road was built, seen on the left of the picture, but the station was never constructed.

COPNOR CROSSING 1986 A bridge was built in 1908, just to the south of the original crossing. The crossing keeper's cottage is still standing, over 75 years after it ceased to be officially used.

BAFFINS POND 1934 When the land in the Baffins area was sold for housing development, the pond was saved for – in the words of the owners – "public pleasure."

(The News)

BAFFINS POND 1986 The pond, with its many birds, is still a pleasure, although the subsequent housing has utilised all the spare land.

STATION ROAD, DRAYTON 1936 Drayton was included in the borough in 1931, and was part of an extremely urban and country-like area. It became very popular with Portsmouth residents who were seeking property away from the crowded city.

(The News)

STATION ROAD, DRAYTON 1986 This picture illustrates exactly how the years can make very little difference to some areas. Apart from the hedges, and the development along Portsdown Hill in the background, the view is almost identical.

COSHAM HIGH STREET 1905 The horse and cart on the left of Waterlooville photographer C.H.T. Marshall's picture stands just outside the old Red Lion inn. The horse-trough around the lamp standard must have made the area a popular stopping place.

(Miss A. Marshall)

COSHAM HIGH STREET 1986 The main road now runs where the old inn stood, and the new Red Lion has been re-sited. New flats and shopping developments have completely changed this part of Cosham.

COSHAM STATION 1905 This picture, another by C.H.T. Marshall, shows the Railway Hotel and the coalyard. Behind the trees on the left is the tram terminus.

(Miss A. Marshall)

COSHAM STATION 1986 The houses on the right of the previous picture are now shops, and the hedgerow has disappeared, but basically the view has changed very little.

PORTSBRIDGE RAILWAY 1936 This view of the railway bridge at Portsbridge, from the ramparts, shows a steam train leaving by the city's only railway approach.

PORTSBRIDGE RAILWAY 1986 The angle is impossible to duplicate today, but this view is close. The motorway and the development in the background, and the demise of steam, all help to bring this picture up to date.

PORTSBRIDGE 1930 This view is taken from the south side of Portsbridge, facing directly towards the camera of the previous picture. A motor-bus and one of the fast-disappearing trams pass each other.

PORTSBRIDGE 1986 This picture was taken from the lower level of the footbridge, itself a legacy of the extra traffic. The site of the original road is now a car park, although the east wall of the bridge still stands, with the lamp standards, but no lamps.

PORTSBRIDGE JUNCTION 1930 A motor-bus is pictured negotiating the roundabout north of Portsbridge, which can be seen in the background. The bridge was opened in 1927 – the commemorative plaque is still to be seen.

(The News)

PORTSBRIDGE JUNCTION 1986 The motorway flyover now dominates the scene. It carries traffic in and out of the city at a scale unheard of in the Thirties.